Becoming a

PRESENT PARENT WORKBOOK

CONNECTING with your CHILDREN in 5 Minutes or Less

Becoming a PRESENT PARENT WORKBOOK

CONNECTING with your CHILDREN in 5 Minutes or Less

Mary Ann Johnson

PLAIN SIGHT PUBLISHING
An imprint of Cedar Fort, Inc.
Springville, Utah

ISBN 13: 978-1-4621-2039-0

Published by Plain Sight Publishing, an imprint of Cedar Fort, Inc.
2373 W. 700 S., Springville, UT 84663
Distributed by Cedar Fort, Inc., www.cedarfort.com

Cover design by Kinsey Beckett

Edited and typeset by Casey Nealon and Jessica Romrell

Printed in the United States of America

10 9 8 7 6 5 4 3 2 1

Printed on acid-free paper

Dedicated to my wonderful children and my grand-children. They have given me the opportunity to practice making changes one small step at a time.

Also by Mary Ann Johnson

Becoming a Present Parent: Connecting with Your Children in 5 Minutes or Less

Becoming a

PRESENT PARENT

Chapter One

How We Check Out

What Is a "Present" Parent?

Objective

Recognize what it means to be "present" and understand eight common ways that dedicated and loving parents unintentionally check out.

Identify your own areas of disengagement.

In order for time with our children to be most effective, it has to be Present' time.

A universal human need is to matter. How successful we are in sending this message is dependent on being able to answer "Yes" to these unspoken questions:

Do you _____________ me?

Do you _____________ me?

Do you _____________ me?

Moms and dads often think they're sending positive, connected messages to their children but what their children are feeling is a major _________________.

Kids measure our love primarily by our attentiveness to them. When we're Present we're attentive. When you know what you're doing and _______________ at your child it says, I ___________________ you, I _______________you, you _____________ to me.

"Presence is more than just being there."
Malcolm Forbes, American Entrepreneur

How Does a Child Ask for Your Presence?

Sweet Marie's Story

The dictionary defines "present" as a gift willingly given without thought of compensation (i.e., unselfishly). That's what I gave to Marie. I gave her the gift of my full attention, my whole self, nothing left on the table. And that's what she needed, for me to be ________________________.

Eight Ways Parents Unknowingly Check Out

1. ______________________________
2. ______________________________
3. ______________________________
4. ______________________________
5. ______________________________
6. ______________________________
7. ______________________________
8. ______________________________

Give It Some Thought

When do you have the most difficulty being "Present" with your child? Is it when you're working, using technology, feeling overwhelmed, or feeling short on time? Is it difficult to be present because you want to fix or because you don't want a mess? Does being Present become difficult when you're asked to play or when you find yourself busy managing your family?

Take some time to honestly think about this issue and list those that are most problematic. Now prioritize them from one to however many items you have on your list, one being the most problematic. Now answer the questions for that one item. How do you react to your child in this situation most of the time? How might it look from your child's point of view, regardless of what your real intention might be? Don't worry about what you need to do to change this behavior; just get these thoughts in writing. Be honest with yourself.

Becoming a

PRESENT PARENT

Chapter Two

The Cost of Checking Out

There Are Costs

Objective

Understand that there are real costs when we check out.

Identify some of the more impactful consequences of checking out.

Determine when you have avoided these consequences.

When we consistently 'check out,' our family pays a ___________________Sometimes the cost of checking out isn't apparent until our children are grown and relationships are not as connected as we would like them to be.

Being Present isn't dependent upon where we work, our finances, the size of our family, our health, our energy level, or anything else. Being Present is a _____.

Six Consequences of Checking Out

1. ______________________________
2. ______________________________
3. ______________________________
4. ______________________________
5. ______________________________
6. ______________________________

"KIDS. They know a BRIBE when they see one. They want a PARENT, not a PAY-OFF. They don't care if you're Jack-King-Rodeo or Mister-You-Own-New-York. All they understand is time spent WITH YOU or WITHOUT YOU. It's that SIMPLE." Carew Papritz, *The Legacy Letters: His Wife, His Children, His Final Gift*

We Can Choose to Be Present!

Elegantly Beautiful

1. Loss of Esteem: We can do all of the ____________ things for our kids but what ultimately matters is how they ___________ when they're with us.

2–3. Poor Parent Response and Poor Parent messages: When we check out, our responses to our children are ___________. Their needs, comments, and behaviors can seem intrusive. They can feel like naughtiness. They can appear overwhelming or excessive. It isn't that they're any of these things, but if our mind is fully____________ it affects how we respond. We unavoidably send the "You Don't Matter" message because poor ___________ lead to poor ______________.

4. Less Enjoyment: The ways we check out often leave us feeling irritated, frustrated, or __________________ by our family members. However, being Present generates feelings of ______________. This feeling reduces the burdens of everyday living. It will increase your ability to manage hard things.

5. Missing What Matters Most: It's funny that the things you can't get back are the easiest to _______________________. Taking three minutes to stop, turn, and take in your child completely means capturing something ________________.

6. Regret: When we check out we will regret the beautiful everyday moments that we missed. We only have our children for about ______________ weeks. Make the most of them!

Give It Some Thought

No matter how you parent now, you have done some things right. But it's easier to remember the things we've done poorly. Focusing on where we error is counter productive. What we focus on we get more of. It's a principle!

Make a list of times when, despite the difficulty, you responded in a Present way. Don't stop until you come up with at least six memories no matter how minor they seem. Write them down in detail. Get another sheet of paper if you need to. Then whenever you feel like you just can't do this, come back to this list and remind yourself that you have done it before and you can do it again.

1. ____________________
2. ____________________
3. ____________________
4. ____________________
5. ____________________
6. ____________________

Becoming a

PRESENT PARENT

Chapter Three

Master Important Skills

Skills to Increase Presence

Objective

Understand that there are skills which, when mastered and used, will help you be Present more often.

Come to believe that being Present isn't as much about time as it is about understanding how to find moments to be Present when we're busy.

Rate yourself on the six PRESENT skills and then try an experiment for one week with each of your children.

1. Active Listening: When we're Present, we hear to __________ with the speaker and to __________ how they feel about what they're saying. It's active and engaged and seeks not only to hear the words but to also hear the ______________.

Steps to Active Listening

a. ______________________________

b. ______________________________

c. ______________________________

d. ______________________________

2. Mini-conversations: The purpose of a mini-conversation is to hear what your kids have to say and also to make a connection that is enjoyable.

Tips for Success

a. ______________________________

b. ______________________________

c. ______________________________

d. ______________________________

e. ______________________________

f. ______________________________

g. ______________________________

h. ______________________________

3. Random Touch: Random touches help reduce the need for ____________, open pathways to __________, and melt stony ______________ and ______________ parents to children.

Types of Random Touches

a. ______________________________

b. ______________________________

c. ______________________________

d. ______________________________

4. Sparks: A spark is anything that a child ________ or _______that lets you know they're interested in something right now.

Burps and Farts
The Water Game

How to See Sparks

a. ______________________________

b. ______________________________

c. ______________________________

5. Play: Make a mental shift about what play needs to look like.

What would be play for you and your child?

____

____

6. Be Silly and Have Fun: Have fun despite the challenges of life.

What do you have in your family right now, that you could do more often, that brings a sense of silliness and fun into your home?

____

____

"We need four hugs a day for survival. We need eight hugs a day for maintenance. We need 12 hugs a day for growth." Virginia Satir, American author and social worker

Give It Some Thought

Do some pondering, meditating, and praying. Which one of these skills feels as if it would make the most difference in your ability to be Present more often? Circle it.

Make a plan to practice this skill. How will you do that? What will it look like? What steps will you take? Write your plan down. Practice the skill you have chosen this week. At the end of the week record how it went. What worked? What didn't work?

On the final page of this workbook you'll find a Master List. Add the skill you're practicing this week to the list. At the end of this class you'll choose one thing from your Master List to focus on for the next few months. When you have a handle on that item you'll return to your Master List and choose the next best thing to work on. You will learn about the importance of choosing the one best thing to work on in lesson six.

- Active listening
- Mini-conversations
- Random touches
- Sparks
- Play
- Be silly and have fun

The Plan: ______________________________

____

____

The Result: ______________________________

____

____

Becoming a

PRESENT PARENT

Chapter Four

Utilize Touchpoints

Touchpoints Connect Us

Objective

Believe that moments of connection can happen during daily activities and require no planning.

Understand what a touchpoint is.

Realize that as you work daily on being Present it will cease to be about what you do for them. It will become how you are when you are with them.

Determine what touchpoint is already working well for you and where to work next.

Touchpoints in a family needn't be something out of the ____________ or planned ______________.

In a family setting, a touchpoint is the point at which one person feels _____________ and _____________ by another person, when they feel they ______________.

Touchpoint moments with children can happen in as little as ________ minutes.

You can have touchpoint moments with your ____________ family at once, as well as one on one.

Children want touchpoint moments with their parents and they know that they can get them during a __________, at ______, and in the ____________.

"By making eye-contact, getting down to your child's level, offering a touch, or using a tone of your voice that conveys a desire to connect genuinely, you disarm yourself. You make it possible to reach your child more deeply and truly move forward together." Hilary Flower, *Adventures in Gentle Discipline: A Parent-to-Parent Guide*

Eight Powerful Touchpoints

1. ______________________________

Seven Reasons for Family Dinner

a. ____________________ e. ____________________
b. ____________________ f. ____________________
c. ____________________ g. ____________________
d. ____________________

2. ______________________________

Bedtime Moments

3. ______________________________

________________ Is Key

Six Tips for Success

a. ____________________ d. ____________________
b. ____________________ e. ____________________
c. ____________________ f. ____________________

4. ______________________________

5.

Transitions with Children and Youth

6.

Six Reasons for Family Night and Meetings

a. d.

b. e.

c. f.

Organizing a Family Night or Meeting

a. f.

b. g.

c. h.

d. i.

e.

7.

Six Reasons to Read as a Family

a. d.

b. e.

c. f.

8.

Give It Some Thought

What Is Working?

What touchpoints are you already using consistently in your home? I am not asking you to list what you are doing perfectly. What I am asking is which of these touchpoints do you implement in your home on a regular basis, knowing that the outcome is sometimes great and other times not? Circle them. It doesn't matter if it is only one or two or even none. No judgment here–just honestly evaluating where you are as a family.

- Family Dinner
- Bedtime
- Car Time
- Family Work/Chores
- Devotional
- Family Night or Meeting
- Family Reading Time
- Transitions

What to Do Next

Think, ponder, and pray about the touchpoints you are not currently using consistently in your home. Which one feels like the next best thing to implement? Circle it. Now add it to your Master List at the back of the workbook.

- Family Dinner
- Bedtime
- Car Time
- Family Work/Chores
- Devotional
- Family Night or Meeting
- Family Reading Time
- Transitions

Try this: Implement the touchpoint you have chosen as the next best thing to try. Do it as many times for one week as you can. If it's dinner, see how many you can have as a family. If it's bedtime see how many times you can give your children three minutes. If it's a transition see how often you can remember to use them to be Present. If it's a family night/meeting have one. There is no goal here. This is an experiment to see how this touchpoint feels to you. How does it feel to your family? Is this really the next best touchpoint to implement? If not, ponder and pray some more and try another one until you are satisfied that you have the next best thing. Then add it to your Master List.

Becoming a

PRESENT PARENT

Chapter Five

Change Your Story

The Truth about Our Stories

Objective

Understand that you *can* control your thoughts and the stories they generate. When you do you will be Present more often.

Believe you're *not* a victim! You have power over your life.

Do the work. Practice controlling your thoughts.

Perspective is an amazing thing. It is, simply put, the ______________ we tell ourselves about what we think is happening in our lives _______, what we believe happened in the ___________, and even what we think will happen in the______.

It all begins with a __________. If we hold it in our minds, it becomes a story because our brain goes to the files and finds ____________ that our thought is correct.

Once we have our story, ______________ are generated. These feelings move us to an ______________ or ____________. Our response produces a _____________, either good or bad.

You change your story by controlling your ___________. You manage your emotions by controlling your _________. When you do this, you take more positive actions and you get better results.

Negative emotions _____________ your ability to choose __________ and____________responses. Positive emotions increase your _________ _______________ by ____________ your mind to more options.

We need to take responsibility for the words we say because our words tell the _____________ story and drive our ____________ and _______________.

"You can't start feeling differently until you start thinking differently."
The Arbinger Institute

We Control the Story

Whether you believe it or not you can control your story no matter what is happening in your life!

The Nine-Year Journey

We are not victims. We can choose how we're going to respond.

You Are Not a Victim

Viktor E. Frankl, a holocaust survivor, said, "When we are no longer able to change a situation—we are challenged to change _________." He reminded us that the one thing that can never be taken from a person is their ability to choose how to _________ and, I would add, their responsibility to mentally write the story that will lead to ______ _________.

Tips for Better Stories:

Tip 1—Take responsibility and stop blaming
Tip 2—Decide to think the best of others
Tip 3—Choose words wisely
Tip 4—Check your core beliefs
Tip 5—Track your thoughts
Tip 6—Teach others what you have learned
Tip 7—Keep practicing

Give It Some Thought

Practice this every day this week. Now add the possibility of using this tool for 30 days to your Mater List. Call it "The 30 Day Taking Control" worksheet.

Use this tool to practice controlling your thoughts. When you have a negative thought, write down the opposite even if it doesn't feel true. All people have weaknesses. I believe they are our strengths in embryo.

Write down your negative thoughts daily. For each negative thought write down the opposite strength and then answer the questions below. Write at least ten thoughts daily. Do this for at 30 days (make 30 copies of this page) and you will begin to see a change in how you feel each day about yourself, your family, your relationships and your life. You will begin taking control.

Date: ______________

1. Strength: ______________
2. Strength: ______________
3. Strength: ______________
4. Strength: ______________
5. Strength: ______________
6. Strength: ______________
7. Strength: ______________
8. Strength: ______________
9. Strength: ______________
10. Strength: ______________

I feel powerful as I manage my thoughts because . . .

I feel confident in clearing out damaging comments because . . .

I feel capable in overcoming negativity because . . .

I feel peaceful in my mind because . . .

Becoming a

PRESENT PARENT

Chapter Six

Do the Simple Things

There Is No Silver Bullet

Objective

Learn that small and simple things, done consistently over time, make all the difference in family success.

Internalize the difference between the 100% devil and the 1% principle.

Decide what you want to change and write it down.

It isn't the big, one-time things that are going to give us __________. It is the __________ things that we do __________ that make all the difference.

This is a ____________ that we can find in legends, in our natural world, taught in religions and self-help books.

It's amazing we ever believe the myth of a silver bullet because the truth of small steps over time has been restated so often. But the myth is __________. It's what we want to believe because the truth is harder to accept.

We would rather do one big thing to change our lives. Although the big thing may take a massive effort on our part, if we gave that effort, then it would be over. However, it is the small steps over time, consistently done, that trip us up. We have to ____________ to do it, set our __________ and then __________ for as long as it takes.

The 100% devil sets us up for failure while the 1% principle guarantees success.

"A remarkable, glorious achievement is just what a long series of unremarkable, inglorious tasks looks like from far away." Tim Urban, American singer-songwriter and actor

We Can Change Our Part of the World!

When we consistently multiply small amounts of time, with small increments of daily effort, we can accomplish magnificent things.

50,000 Daffodils

Whenever you hear about someone who's achieved an extraordinary goal rarely, if ever, do you hear about the process they used–small steps taken consistently, over time.

Naaman and the Wise Servant

The __________ is the enemy of this true principle—small things, consistently done over time, brings BIG results. He tells you everything has to be fixed now, there isn't enough __________, you have to do it ____________ or not at all; there is so much to do you will never get it done.

However, the ____________ will make the biggest difference because it puts exponential growth on your side.

Stop Complaining!

Give It Some Thought

Doing the same actions over and over again isn't easy. We live in a quick fix world. We want it NOW. But we need to throw out the 100% devil and embrace the 1% principle. So how can you sustain the effort needed to do the best 1% for the time it takes to see success?

1. Concentrate on the one thing you need to do right now.
2. Commit to be consistent for as long as it takes.
3. Remember that being consistent is not the same as being perfect.
4. Break what you want into smaller steps.
5. Create space for change.
6. Keep your word.
7. Make sure that your steps are about you and not others.
8. Focus on today only—that is all you have to work with.
9. Believe the end result will be exponential growth.

What have you thought about changing or doing in the past year to improve yourself or your family? What matters most? Write it down. Ponder, meditate, or pray about your list and which item is most important, the best 1%. Add this to the Master List on the last page of this workbook.

1. ____________________
2. ____________________
3. ____________________
4. ____________________
5. ____________________
6. ____________________
7. ____________________

Becoming a

PRESENT PARENT

Chapter Seven

Know What You Want

How Does Your Family Feel?

Objective

Understand that knowing what you want can help you become a more Present parent.

Realize that flying by the seat of your pants is a poor way for a family to travel.

Do the work – write it down!

When you know what you want and your family begins to feel the way you want, you have more motivation to ____________.

When your family knows where they're headed they'll be more willing to be ____________________.

Running a family is somewhat like running a business or organization. Good desires will not make either one ___________.

A successful family _____________doesn't just happen. We have to have a clear _____ and then do the ______.

To know what you want you have to think and talk about it. Then you need to ask yourself good questions. When you're ready, work with your family to create a ______________________________.

No matter the make up of your family, a clear statement of your intent helps you get what you want.

Families who fly by the seat of their pants ___________ more.

"A problem only exists if there is a difference between what is actually happening and what you desire to be happening."
Kenneth H. Blanchard

How to Know What You Want

1. Think about what you want and talk it over.

2. Ask good questions:
- What are the values we want our family to embody?
- What's the "feeling" we want in our household?
- In what activities or items will we invest our time and money?
- What words will best describe our family?
- What words would we like our kids to use to describe our family? What words would they use to describe our family right now?
- What are our strengths as a family?
- What do we feel our family is called to do?
- What do we want our family legacy to be?
- What does our family stand for?
- What principles should guide decisions? Are they the same for both individuals and the family unit?
- How will religion or spirituality look in our family?
- What is our family economy?

Crystallize What You Stand For

3. Use the process:
- The parents talk among themselves about what is important to them. Work out any differences. Have a united front.
- The parents tell their children about these values.
- The entire family discusses the values so that everyone understands them.
- Help family members "buy in" or "take ownership" for the statement.
- Parents make the final decisions. You know what is best. Children can contribute with their ideas that should be treated as valuable, but you make the final decisions.
- Make changes as they are needed until it is just what you want. This takes time. As you recite it, you will feel if anything needs to be adjusted.

Give It Some Thought

When you're ready, here are some assignments that will help you move through the process of creating your Family Mission Statement. Add creating a FMS to the last page of this workbook. At the end of the class you will choose one thing from your Master List to begin working on.

Assignment #1: Try a brainstorming exercise by asking yourself: what are the core things I want my child to do or know? Put your list on the following page so you can add to it when things come to your mind.

Assignment #2: What roadblocks, if any, have been keeping your family from creating your Family Mission Statement? Are these barriers real or excuses? If they are real, write them down. Now begin considering solutions to these roadblocks. If you need help reach out to someone you know who uses an FMS or do some research on the Internet to help you begin seeing opportunities and solutions.

Assignment #3: Make a plan for what activities you will use to prime your family's pump of creativity, which questions you will ask, and which form you want your mission statement to take. Then determine your timeline. As you develop your plan, give particular attention to making these activities fun and memorable. Include food, outings, or whatever will make the events special for your family.

Assignment #4: Organize your thoughts. Get them into concrete form by writing them down as a family. No wordsmithing. Just get all the thoughts down on paper. Then assign someone to create the final draft. Unveil it to your family. Make it an occasion!

Assignment #5: Use it.

- Recite it daily.
- Use it to help make big decisions.
- Use it to help regain focus and realignment with the things that matter most to your family.
- Use it to guide your family educational plan. The specific values that your FMS mentions, such as money management, entrepreneurialism, freedom, honesty, or service can all inform your educational opportunities, ideas, and materials.
- Have fun with it. Have your children create artwork or collages that reflect your final mission statement.

NOTES

Assignment #1: What are the core things I want my child to do or know?

Assignment #2: Roadblocks

Becoming a

PRESENT PARENT

Chapter Eight

Make It about Them

Outcome vs. Process

Objective

Understand that adults and kids approach things differently and it impacts our ability to be Present.

Hidden motives can change how we are when we work with kids.

Journal what your experience has been–what you want it to be.

One of the biggest differences in kids and adults is that kids are ____________ driven, and adults are ______________ driven.

It's more difficult to remain Present if what you're doing with your kids is ultimately about ___________ and not ____________.

Keeping your mind on the child and the joy they're experiencing will help you have far more __________________ in just about everything you do with your kids and family.

Our _________________, even hidden ones, can color our experience and make it challenging to be Present with our children.

"Process—It's all about the engagement, the exploration, the experiment. The joie-de-vivre. The moment at hand. The immediate feedback. Process, by its very definition is an 'open-ended' experience. It's you and the media, and there are no right or wrong answers. It's literally: go with the flow and see what happens. It's quite possibly messy. Even TOTALLY messy! It's very often exciting. It's inherently personal: process. It's a moment-by-moment, PLAY-by-PLAY (get it?) unfolding with the material, the medium, the moment."
Debbie Clement

Motives Matter

1. ______________________________

Our expectations can suck the joy out of an experience.

2. ______________________________

Let a sense of satisfaction and happiness for being with our family be the reward.

3. ______________________________

The natural state of children is messiness.

4. ______________________________

Choose the relationship over the look of the finished product or outcome.

5. ______________________________

Let it be about them and not about you.

6. ______________________________

See children's projects differently, then you'll know the right use of materials.

The Boat and the Robot

7. ______________________________

If they don't enjoy the process, then it doesn't fill their need.

8. ______________________________

T-I-M-E says loud and clear. "You are on my list, you matter to me."

Give It Some Thought

Take a moment to journal your experience when working with your children. How does it feel? How do you feel? How do your kids end up feeling? Be honest with yourself. After you have written your feelings, distill out your motives. Once we know what something is, we can change it.

Becoming a

PRESENT PARENT

Chapter Nine

Adjust Your Approach

Management vs. Relationship

Objective

Understand that adults and kids approach things differently and it impacts our ability to be Present.

Hidden motives can change how we are when we work with kids.

Journal what your experience has been—what you want it to be.

Being Present with our children should be our ultimate __________ rather than ticking things off of our list.

When we're Present with our children even ___________ give us an opportunity to practice.

When we're stuck in the ______________ we will find it harder to be successful as a family. We need to spend more time ______ our family rather than _________ our family.

Using the 1% principle helps us step out of the day-to-day ________ of our family, and spend more time working on our family relationships.

It takes more thought to be Present than it does time. Make being Present a _______. Let it become ________ you are with your children.

When you're engaged with your child, just be right here, right now. All we have is ___________. That is all we have ever had. We can fill it with _____________ or we can make room for relationship. It's a _________.

"It's so easy to get lost in the responsibilities of parenting that we forget to actually enjoy the journey!"
Sumitha Bhandarkar, *A Fine Parent*

The Payoff for Adjusting Your Approach

1. ______________________________

2. ______________________________

3. ______________________________

4. ______________________________

The Door, the Father, the Boy

5. ______________________________

The 111-Year-Old Mom

6. ______________________________

What Will You TREASURE Most?

Please, Just Look at Me!

Give It Some Thought

Where do you get stuck in the "doin' it," "doin' it," "doin' it"? What parts of your day do you find most challenging to be Present? Make a list. Remember John and his bedroom.

Now pick **one** item from your list that you think is most important, the best 1%. Come up with an experiment to get out of the 'doin' it,' and get into the relationship with the one item you have chosen. Add the item you picked to your master list. This week play with your experiment. Remember that it's an experiment to see how it makes you feel, how it makes your child feel, and how it impacts the relationship. Try it out for one week.

1. ____

What you will do to be Present

____

____

2. ____

What you will do to be Present

____

____

3. ____

What you will do to be Present

____

____

Becoming a

PRESENT PARENT

Chapter Ten

Remember: Less Is More

The Cost of Raising Kids

Objective

Understand that the real cost of raising kids is giving them your Presence, not things.

Learn that stuff both physical and non-physical steals your time and energy.

Determine how you can simplify for greater energy and Presence.

__________ kids are happy kids!

There's a cost to connecting with kids but it isn't money, vacations, or things. It's __________.

The Poppy Principle—When we pay the real price of raising kids then we create __________ that connect us.

Studies show the number one element to happiness for kids and youth is ________.

Things of the _____________ always trump things of the _____________.

Keeping It Simple

When we simplify our ___________ stuff, our ____________ stuff, and our ________ stuff, we free up ___________ and __________.

Stop using your only actual possession, __________, for managing stuff.

"It is amazing to me that most things I remember from my childhood make me smile and happy, considering that we had really little money, a lot of empty stomachs and much reason to pray for help. I had a wonderful childhood, not because of the things we had but because we had each other." Desirée Campbell

What Else Makes Kids Happy?

1. ______________________________
2. ______________________________
3. ______________________________
4. ______________________________
5. ______________________________
6. ______________________________
7. ______________________________

Move, Move, Move!

Why we hang on to stuff

1. ______________________________
2. ______________________________
3. ______________________________
4. ______________________________
5. ______________________________

Give It Some Thought

Look at the list of things that make for happy kids and families. Pick one item from the list that you think would make the most difference if your family embraced it. Write it down. Now think, ponder, meditate or pray about this one thing. How could you incorporate it into your family more often? Let's say you picked happy parent. What small step could you take toward being happier? More sleep. Eating better. Exercise. Being Present more often. Now write in detail the one step you will take. For example—I will go to bed 30 minutes earlier three times each week for the next month. Add this item to your Master List.

Item ______________________

The step I will take ______________________

Cleaning out our physical stuff, our emotional house, or our calendar can be daunting. So let's take it slow. Make a list of the things that feel extra heavy to you: too many dishes, clothes, a full garage. List any old wounds or negative emotions you are hanging on to. List anything on your calendar that feels burdensome. Ponder your list. Is there anything you feel you can take one step toward lightening? Maybe it's the utensil drawer, maybe cutting out one extracurricular activity. Maybe it's forgiving someone. Add this one thing to your Master List.

Becoming a

PRESENT PARENT

Chapter Eleven

Turn Away from Technology

A Pandora's Box

Objective

Be clear that technology takes a toll on families.

Understand that technology is often addictive but can be managed.

Determine how your family will keep technology in the right place in your family—which is never before the family.

How can I __________ technology so that it doesn't negatively impact my home and family?

Technology can be _____________. We can become addicted to the __________ of using technology even when there is no __________.

Technology lacks the kind of natural __________ that help us moderate other activities.

When parents ____________ their technology use, they are usually amazed at how much time they give to it. They also usually admit that this loss of time is taking its toll on their ________________ and ________________.

"Technology . . . is a queer thing. It brings you great gifts with one hand, and it stabs you in the back with the other."
C.P. Snow, *New York Times*, 15 March 1971

What Is the Toll of Unmanaged Use?

1. ______________________________
2. ______________________________
3. ______________________________
4. ______________________________

The Little Brats!

Keeping Technology in Its Place

1. ______________________________
2. ______________________________
3. ______________________________
4. ______________________________
5. ______________________________
6. ______________________________
7. ______________________________

Give It Some Thought

Take an honest look at your use of technology as a family. Where do you see it causing problems? Write them down. Ponder, pray, or meditate on the list you have made. What one item seems to be what you should work on? Put a star by it. Now determine one small step you can take to get this in the right place in your family. Using the item you have chosen and the step you are prepared to take, write out your experiment. Add this experiment to your Master List. When you are ready to work on it, follow through for two weeks. Then evaluate how it worked. If you need to, adjust your experiment and give it another try.

The Experiment

The Evaluation

Becoming a

PRESENT PARENT

Chapter Twelve

Caring for Self = Better Presence

An Investment in Family

Objective

Recognize that caring for yourself is an investment in your family.

Accept that you cannot get away enough to get all the self-care you need.

Learn to care for yourself right where you are.

Self-care and having children are not mutually ________________.

Self-care helps parents maintain __________, facilitates __________, and staves off taking our ____________ out on our children. Self-care helps us remain freer of _____________, exhaustion, or feeling _________. It keeps us ________.

We all use __________ as our reason to neglect ourselves.

When we take full responsibility for how our lives look we stop __________ people, circumstances, money, or time.

Self-care is an ____________ in your family.

"Self care is never a selfish act–it is simply good stewardship of the only gift I have, the gift I was put on earth to offer to others."
Parker Palmer, author, educator, and activist

Seven Ways to Care for Self

1. ______________________________

2. ______________________________

3. ______________________________

4. ______________________________

Six ways to put down emotional weight

a.	d.
b.	e.
c.	f.

5. ______________________________

6. ______________________________

Three Experiments

7. ______________________________

You are going to spend far more time with your children than you are going to spend without them, so it's imperative to learn how to do a little self-care while you are in the thick of parenting. When you care for yourself you care for your family.

Give It Some Thought

Make a list of things that feel nurturing to you that you can have at home: reading, taking a walk, having a cup of tea, more sleep, eating at the table, writing, painting, etc. Now think about how and when you can add these small elements to your life. Pick one thing from your list that appeals to you the most. How could you make that happen more regularly? Come up with an experiment. Add the experiment to your Master List. When you are ready to work on this, do your experiment for one week and then evaluate how it is going. Make any adjustments that you need to and try again.

The Experiment

The Evaluation

Becoming a

PRESENT PARENT

Chapter Thirteen

Blessed Are Your Eyes for They See—A Summary

You Can Do This

Objective

Understand that we all parent in our lifetime–even if we have no children of our own.

Know that being Present is how we need to be to have the best possible relationships.

Believe that no matter how you are currently parenting you aren't doing as badly as you think!

The nature of families helps us to want to become our ____________ selves. It is a laboratory of ______________.

It doesn't matter how long you have been __________, a few months or many years. It doesn't matter the ____________ of your children. It doesn't even matter if you have never had _____________. We all parent and we all continue to parent for our entire lives.

Despite how it may look or feel you aren't doing as badly as you think. Children are resilient. But we can all do better. We need to pick the best 1% and begin.

When we learn to be Present as our day unfolds, no matter what it dishes out to us, it completely changes our responses to our children and positively impacts our relationship with them.

"But blessed are your eyes, for they see: and your ears, for they hear."
Matthew 13:16

"When we are Present, even if it's only a few times a week, a few minutes at a time, we will be blessed to 'see' and 'hear' in an extraordinary way." Mary Ann Johnson

A Few Final Thoughts

I know that no matter where you are in your parenting strengths or weakness, you can get better at being Present. As you do, it will make a difference in your family relationships and your level of happiness.

A Life-Changing Moment

The Honey Test

The Key to Happiness

Our homes are the perfect place to practice the art of being Present. When we are Present with our children we send the clear and important message, I hear you. I see you. I will love you. You matter to me.

There is no silver bullet to family success. It takes time and Presence.

Give It Some Thought

We have covered a lot of ground. It is imperative that you remember the difference between the 100% devil and the 1% principle. One leads to frustration and mediocre results and the other leads to success. Pick one thing to work on; the 1% you feel called to do. Then when you have had some success with that one thing, pick another.

Look at the Master List you have made of possible ways to move forward in your family relationships. Now ponder, pray, and meditate. Pick the one thing you will begin working on today. Just one. Your family will not "go to the garbage dump" if you don't work on everything now. Break your best 1% into smaller steps and begin. I promise that as you take one step at a time, consistently over time you will accomplish enough.

Remember that success comes as we take small consistent steps over time.

The 1% that you will begin working on today

____

____

"But blessed are your eyes, for they see: and your ears, for they hear." Matthew 13:16

Master List

At the end of the course you will choose one, and only one, item from your Master List to begin working on. When you feel that you have made good progress with that one thing, return to the list and choose one more thing. I know this will feel slow. I get it! However, you will increase your chances of making BIG changes in the happiness level of yourself and your family if you remember the value of making 1% improvements and the failure that comes when we let the 100% devil rule.

Remember that success comes as we take small consistent steps over time.

Notes

Scan to visit

www.becomingapresentparent.com